The Principles of Prophecy

David C Bates

Copyright © 2023 David C Bates

All rights reserved. This book is protected by the copyright laws of the United States of America. This book may not be copied or reprinted for commercial gain or profit. The use of short quotations or occasional page copying for personal or group study is permitted and encouraged. Permission will be granted upon request.

ISBN: 9798387699412

DEDICATION

This book is dedicated to my lovely wife Michelle, my beautiful daughters, my handsome son-in-laws, and my adventurous grandchildren who all have influenced me and helped me become the man I am. Poppi loves you!

CONTENTS

	Endorsements	vii
1	What is Prophecy	1
2	Purposes of Prophecy	5
3	Who Can Prophesy	13
4	How do you Prophesy	15
5	How does God Speak	20
6	Interpretation	36
7	Prophetic Protocols	52
8	Contending for Words	62
9	Tested in the Prophetic	81
10	Closing	86
11	Prophetic Exercises	87

ENDORSEMENTS

You're going to love this book! There has been a lot of unbiblical teaching, distortions by self-promoters, and many churches 'turned off' to the prophetic because of misunderstanding, even bad experiences, etc. In this book, David Bates clears the air. 1 Cor. 14:31 and vs. 33 assure us, "For you can all prophesy one by one, so that all may learn and all be encouraged," v. 33 "For God is not a God of confusion but of peace."

David has such a heart of love. I have known David and his wife Michelle for over ten years and can say everyone who meets them comes away much better than before they knew them. You will too. I invite you to have them speak at your church, conference, or business group.

The Father's heart is evident in this foundational manual everyone should read to draw closer to the Lord's love, grow in intimacy, and hunger for all the Lord gives us freely through the death, burial, and resurrection of Jesus Christ. When we know our supernatural identity in Christ, His peace which passes all understanding, also gives us the power to destroy the works of the enemy of our soul. Do you want that in your own life and family?

You can learn the life-changing foundations of the prophetic found throughout the Bible. Many who read this book will encounter the refreshing presence of the fullness of the Lord, which He designed for us to walk in. In an age of many deceptions, many are looking for hope, truth, and love only found in our Creator and His love letter to us, the Bible.

David shares powerful testimonies with deeply personal experiences of lives blessed and changed through his many years of ministry, teaching, and bringing healing to thousands, both physical and spiritual healing.

You will be strengthened and encouraged to dream big with God as you learn from the revelation the Lord has shown David regarding the prophetic with many supporting scriptural proofs, written in a very understandable and relevant way that draws you into mastery. You will read many of the touching stories to see how you, too, can draw closer to the Lord in this systematic, loving way that you will be able to partner with the Lord in every area of your life and learn how 'we may all prophesy' and bring heaven to earth in our lives, family and those you interact with.

Get ready for a life-changing read you have been waiting to see and experience!

Jorge Parrott, Ph.D.
President of CMM.world and CMMTheology.org
Fort Mill, SC

David's book, *The Principles of Prophecy*, is an essential resource for anyone who wants to truly live out a life of love with the Lord Jesus. Many minister out of motives that focus on pleasing others, not the Lord. David's teaching establishes prophetic ministry upon the foundation of Jesus Christ, which flows both in the power and wisdom of the Holy Spirit. *The Principles of Prophecy* trains us to lead others to encounter Jesus through prophecy, but also grows us in grace as we are transformed by the word of the Lord. This is a must-read book!

John Heiss
Pastor of Wellspring Fellowship Church
President, Oxbow Ministries
Martinsville, VA

I have known David Bates as a dear friend and brother in Christ for several years. I love the clarity and wisdom he brings to the table in helping cultivate the prophetic gift. We need leaders and teachers in the body of Christ that live what they preach. David is such a man. I have written and read many book on prophetic ministry, and I highly value the contents and simplicity within the pages of David's book. I highly recommend *The Principles of Prophecy* to anyone aspiring to grow in hearing the voice of God. Well done, David!

Ruth Mangicapre
Founder of The Southeast Prophetic Network
High Point, NC

For the world to function as God intends, God must have a people on the earth who know not only how to hear the voice of God but to speak for God on the planet. In *The Principles of Prophecy*, my friend David Bates has written a practical manual to equip the body with the basics of prophetic ministry. This is not simply a book to read but one that biblically guides you into experiencing and moving in the gift of prophecy as God intended. I commend to you this manual and the ministry of David Bates.

Abner Suarez, International Speaker and Author
For Such A Time As This, Inc.
Dunn, NC

1 WHAT IS PROPHECY

Prophecy is <u>hearing</u> a message from God, and then <u>delivering</u> that message to the audience it was intended for.

Prophecy is comprised of two parts - *hearing* and *sharing*. When we receive a revelation from God, we are "hearing" what God is showing us. *How* we hear, *what* we hear, and *the accuracy* of our hearing are critical aspects to ensure that we receive the revelation as God intended.

The second critical element is delivering, or sharing, the message. Typically, we would speak this message to the intended audience. While speaking would normally be our delivery method, there are other ways we can deliver God's message. For example, Old Testament prophets acted out messages God gave based on God's instruction to them, such as the time when Jeremiah went and hid some clothing items in the bank of a river and then pulled them out. Or another time, when Hosea was instructed to go marry a woman.

Prophecy can be foretelling or forth-telling.

Throughout the Old Testament prophecy is given in two modes, foretelling and forth-telling. Foretelling means simply to predict the future. Forth-telling means to publish or broadcast a message. Prophets operated in both of these modes when giving messages to their audience.

Some great examples of foretelling include the messianic prophecies in the Old Testament which told about events that Jesus would do and where he would come from. Prophets foretold that the messiah would be a Nazarene, he would be born in Bethlehem, and he would enter Jerusalem riding on a donkey. Several hundred details about Jesus were recorded in the messianic prophecies.

Most people think that prophecy is focused only on predicting the future, although careful study of the scripture reveals that God had prophets speak messages that focused on issues other than the future. As prophets, Isaiah, Jeremiah, and Ezekiel shared several forth-telling messages to Israel, calling them back to serving God and to leave their idolatry behind.

Forth-telling focuses on expressing God's heart and his thoughts, and will often speak about present conditions and circumstances from God's point of view. It provides us a glimpse from his perspective.

In many of the passages in Isaiah, Jeremiah, and Ezekiel there is sometimes a mixture of foretelling and forth-telling that occurs when they were prophesying and speaking to Israel. A great example of them switching between these two modes of prophecy is in the first chapter of Isaiah. In this chapter Isaiah expresses a message the Lord gave to him regarding Judah and Jerusalem. The first part of the message, in verses 2-23, Isaiah operates in a forth-telling mode and speaks about how God sees the rebellious way in which the nation was living before God, and how God was rebuking them for their waywardness and calling them back to Himself. This is forth-telling prophecy, which is distinguished in that there is no discussion in several of these verses about the future; it is just describing God's heart and calling people back to himself. It is also not a doctrinal message, but rather a heartfelt appeal to Judah to turn back to God and how God sees their current condition. Then, in verses 24-31, the message shifts to foretelling and discusses what God will do in the future for Judah.

It's important to understand these two modes of prophesying as there will be times where you will operate in foretelling and then forth-telling or even both when sharing a message the Lord has given you for another person. Prophecy does not just focus on predicting the future.

Why Does Prophecy Exist?

When God created the universe, He had a blank

canvas. There was no existing format or design. He made everything and created everything according to His good pleasure and based on His own counsel.

God could have created anything and one of the things He chose to create was the gift of prophecy. Prophecy is a means for God to communicate to His creation. Prophecy communicates the secrets of God's heart. He made a way to speak to man so that there would be no confusion or misunderstanding. Why? Because God really loves people!

People desperately need clear messages of God's love. In its purest form, prophecy projects both a message of reconciliation and a message of the love that flows from the Father's heart. These messages are so urgently needed in our world that is filled with messages of fear, condemnation, anxiety, judgement and uncertainty. And, in an age where people are looking everywhere for a sense of acceptance, identity, and meaning, those who have a relationship with our loving Abba Father carry the solution to this crisis. The solution's name is the Holy Spirit. He lives inside of born-again believers (John 14:17), He wants to use us to be God's mouthpiece, telling the world that God really is for them, and not against them.

2 PURPOSES OF PROPHECY

Prophesy broadcasts good news

We know one of the purposes of prophetic messages is that God desires to see people strengthened, encouraged, and their hearts comforted, as this is highlighted to us in Corinthians 14:3. That is good news we get to share!

The book of Corinthians also illuminates to us that God has plans of peace to prosper us and to give us a future. This passage also agrees with the message in Jeremiah 29. This is also good news!

From these passages, along with weighing the balance of prophetic ministry we read in scripture, it can be concluded that the goal of prophecy is to lead a person into a *better* position with God, whether it be a call to reconciliation, or an invitation to a deeper relationship and journey with God.

Revelations 19:10b tells us that the testimony of Jesus

is the spirit of prophecy. Jesus's testimony was a life sacrificed to reconcile men to God. He lived redemption! Operating in this same spirit, true prophetic ministry will always have redemption as the primary motive. This is not just redemption of salvation, but God redeeming every aspect and every area of our lives. We are all in the process of being conformed into the image of Christ, so that means every area of our life can be redeemed to reflect him.

As we prophesy, the heart of those we speak with should become drawn to the Lord. This is why those who prophesy must themselves be actively engaged in intimacy with God. We minister out of what we possess. How can you encourage others to become one with Jesus if you are estranged in your heart toward Him? John 15 shows us that abiding in the place of close communion is the only way to be fruitful.

Jesus taught many things while on the earth, but one of His primary missions was to reveal the Father to us. In reply to Philip's desire to see the Father (John 14:8-9), Jesus asked "How is it that you have not seen Him? If you have seen me, then you have seen the Father." As we go deeper into prophetic ministry, we should begin reflecting the image of our Father in heaven. Jesus testified of who the Father was...this is the spirit of prophecy. And that is good news, because God is good!

The Prophetic binds up broken hearts

Life on the earth is filled with brokenness. It enters

human hearts on so many levels and in several ways. Jesus came to the earth filled with grace and truth (John 1:17). His attitude toward broken men is a tangible sign that he was filled with and overflowed in grace; and his truth was the antidote to heal the brokenness.

Jesus came in grace, which means unmerited favor. This grace is a primary attribute of love. 1 Corinthians 13 shows us that love bears all things, love is not self-seeking, and love does not think evil. Grace and love are interested in one thing – repairing, redeeming, and patching up that which is broken.

I remember once ministering in a country where we had been prophesying for several days and after so many hundreds of words, I came to find my limitation. I was burnt out. Yet there were still more wanting ministry! In that moment of coming to my end, I found a new well of prophetic revelation! It's called love! In my moment of weakness, I found the Lord encouraging me to see these people as He sees them. I found love in a whole new way. As I submitted to love, fresh revelation came to my heart for those before me.

When we operate in grace and love, we see things differently. We have vision for possibilities, and we see beauty regardless of obvious flaws. A great example of this is the woman caught in adultery recorded in John 8:3-11. The Pharisees saw the woman through the lenses of her sin and wanted to stone her. But Jesus saw something they didn't see - a life that was broken and needed encouragement. She needed a father-daughter moment of counsel to help her get back on the right track.

People know that they are sinful. They are aware of their mistakes. Most people live with a truckload of guilt and shame and regret. ***What they don't know is that God loves them and gave all for them.*** The price that Jesus paid to redeem us from the cost of our mistakes illustrates the tremendous value He places on people. The prophetic speaks to the value that God sees in others and draws people out of shame and regret. The prophetic releases healing to broken hearts.

The Prophetic releases truth - setting captives free

1 John 3:8b shows us that Jesus appeared on the earth to destroy the works of the devil. The word translated "destroy" is the Greek word *lyo* (pronounced luo). In the King James Version of the Bible this same word is also translated as '*loosing any person or thing tied or bound*'. So, the life of Jesus was given to tear down what the enemy had built and to bring freedom to those who were held captive to lies, bondages, and anything that interfered with relationship with God. The primary goal of our enemy is to tie us up in a web of lies so that we are deaf to truth. If the enemy can succeed in creating an environment where deception rules, then his influence reigns in that environment.

We live in a time when that which is evil is called good and that which is good is called evil. A great example of this is the abortion movement in the United States. Those who argue for having the option to abort children think that the right to choose is more important than having the right to live. Restricting choice in their mind is evil, while having choice is good. And yet many of these same activists will protest about putting in an oil pipeline because they're worried about a turtle species potentially dying. Their actions and words place more value on the lives of turtles than on human babies that are designed in the image of God. This is the epitome of deception!

I've given so many words over the years regarding God's thoughts toward a person that I've lost count. And I've seen so many get delivered from deception. One example that I'll never forget was during ministry in a small church in Virginia. I was with a team who was prophesying to the entire church, one by one. It came down to the last woman who was standing waiting for a word. She was in her 60's. I heard a phrase for her, and it was "You are beautiful!" I was obedient to the message I felt like God was emphasizing to her, so I began to prophesy to her about her beauty and what God saw. She just began weeping. Later that evening she told me the rest of the story. When she was 12 years old her dad stood her up in a crowded room of people and told her to her face that she was ugly! That had left such a horrible scar on her soul. And when I spoke this over her publicly, all those years of pain came flooding to the surface and were released. She finally got freedom from that painful scar and lie.

The prophetic gifting at its highest function releases God's perspective to the world and those around us. Understanding how He views the world and those that surround us, how He sees the past, the present, and the future, will liberate us from deception. His viewpoint provides clarity where confusion existed, healing to pain, and creates order in place of chaos.

Prophecy announces the time and place of favor

Behind every prophetic word the intention of the Father is revealed. For a person, He reveals the next area of their upgrade. For a nation, He indicates where He is releasing grace or calling them into purpose. For a group or church, He is indicating the place of blessing and calling them into destiny. All of these words are pointing to a fundamental action...the Lord is indicating where He is releasing favor. Many times this favor and grace is declared and released to create that which does not currently exist.

Jeremiah 29 is a great illustration of this principle. In Jeremiah 29, God tells Israel that He has plans for them to give them future and a hope. Yet they were in bondage at that moment, carried into captivity by the Babylonians. He tells them to plant vineyards and raise children and learn to seek Him in the land of Babylon until He brings them back to their own land. God was indicating to them where His favor was for their life for that time and season. He was giving them instruction on how they could make their time fruitful and agree with God's purposes in this season of their life.

The prophetic releases words of destiny, pointing to favor and gives the receiver opportunity to look beyond their past and present circumstances. It provides vision and hope to move beyond and to go up higher.

It's so important to understand where God's favor for our lives is being released. We only have so much time and energy. With our limited resources, It's so important to know where we should invest them to get success. Prophetic words indicate where God is pointing to favor for our lives. He's showing us where to invest to get the highest return. I'm not talking about money, but spiritual currency. God wants us to get the highest return in heaven's currency...to become rich toward God.

Prophecy brings direction and correction

First Corinthians 14:3 shows us that prophecy speaks exhortation. The Greek word used here is *paraklesis*. The word exhort means to give a message with urgency; encouraging someone to do something; or give warning or advice. We see this type of prophetic messaging throughout the scripture. *Paraklesis* was also used in several ways including to admonish, intreat, or beseech. These are all words meaning to give a message with urgency, encouraging the listener to action that is important to their livelihood.

In this book we emphasize the need to operate with the same heart that Jesus had. He encouraged those around Him to be reconciled to God. The spirit of true prophecy is not to expose, condemn, and judge, but rather to reconcile. We want to operate with the same spirit that Jesus operated with, which means our motive is to bring people back to God. Will there be times when a person prophesying reveals hidden sin? That could happen, but the motive of doing this should be to restore right relationship with God, never to condemn a person. And it should be done in the right protocol. Much more can be said about this in later sections of this book.

3 WHO CAN PROPHESY

According to 1 Corinthians 14:31 everyone can prophesy. This scripture states *"For you can all prophesy one by one, that all may learn and all may be encouraged."* And in 1 Corinthians 14:1 Paul encourages the church to pursue spiritual gifts, especially to prophesy. So, we can see in these two verses not only can everyone prophesy, but we are encouraged to pursue this ability. Why is this emphasized by the Holy Spirit who inspired these thoughts? Because this gifting has the capacity to heal, deliver, unlock, create vision, and empower people to their destiny.

Were these thoughts expressed by Paul the first time God had this in mind? No, this is not the first time. In fact, when God created man in the beginning, He created them in His image. In other words, He expected men and women to be an expression of the image of God. This expression would include the capability to speak with the intention and thoughts that originate from God's heart.

In Joel 2 the scripture declares *"and it shall be in the last days,"* God says, *"that I will pour forth of my spirit on all mankind; and your sons and your daughters shall prophesy, and your young men shall see visions, and your old men shall dream dreams; even on my bondslaves, both men and women, I will in those days pour forth of my spirit and they shall prophesy."*

So who can prophesy? Anyone can. The intention in Joel 2, Genesis, Acts, and 1 Corinthians 14 is to show that anyone can prophesy. It's always been this way, and it's always been God's intention for all to speak with His voice. In fact, one day the whole earth will be filled with God's glory which includes declaring and speaking the thoughts and words inspired by God.

4 HOW DO YOU PROPHESY

The act of prophesying has two primary elements - hearing from God and then sharing what He shows you.

God can initiate speaking to you or you can ask Him to speak to you. There are times noted in the scripture where God initiated the interaction with prophets by giving them a dream, a vision, or some other supernatural encounter. And there are times where prophets approached God and asked Him to speak, give direction, or provide them insight. In either way, the main element we see is that God speaks and then we share what He shows.

If God is initiating the contact, then we simply must recognize when He is showing us things and then act on them. In other moments and ministry times, we may need to initiate the contact with God, so we should practice <u>asking, listening, and then acting</u> on what He shows us to do.

Asking

We can have confidence in approaching God to ask Him to speak to us as Luke 11:10-13 instructs. In this scripture we are taught that <u>everyone who asks receives.</u> There are two dynamics that need to be in place for this to work. I need to ask, and I need to be confident He will speak. When one or both dynamics aren't functioning there is a breakdown, and the result is that discouragement can set in. Asking and then expecting both require faith. We must believe God will speak, and more than that, He wants to speak to you.

How can we guard our heart against doubt and unbelief - these two archenemies of faith? We must believe first that God is good and He wants to give us good things. The goodness of God has been a debate since the beginning of the garden of Eden. Remember when Satan came to Eve and talked to her about the tree they weren't supposed to eat from? Satan approached Eve by questioning the goodness of God - asserting that God was trying to withhold something that would actually make Eve and Adam's life better. When Eve accepted this argument, she stepped into doubt, ate from disobedience, and ended in separation. Doubt of His goodness keeps us in the land of separation.

Hebrews 11:6 tells us that anyone who comes to God must believe first that He exists and secondly that He rewards those who diligently seek Him. The connotation of diligence is that we are pursuing Him without doubt, or in other words we are all in. What I have learned over the years, is that if I ask God to speak to me, He will. Luke 11 reminds us that we have a good Father who wants to interact with us, wants to bless us with good things, and wants to speak to us when we approach Him.

For everyone who asks, receives; and he who seeks, finds; and to him who knocks, it will be opened. "Now suppose one of you fathers is asked by his son for a fish; he will not give him a snake instead of a fish, will he? Or if he is asked for an egg, he will not give him a scorpion, will he? If you then, being evil, know how to give good gifts to your children, how much more will your heavenly Father give the Holy Spirit to those who ask Him?" (Luke 11:10-13).

Listening

The second part that has to be present for us to operate prophetically, is that we have to listen for God. We ask God to speak, then we must listen for His answer. John 10:27 reminds us that God's sheep hear His voice and follow Him. In this scripture we have a promise that we can hear God. While you go through this journey of learning to hear God, be encouraged that God has made provision for you to have this ability.

The act of listening is more than just waiting to hear something with your physical sense of hearing. As we will study later in this book, God speaks and gives revelation through many different methods. He can reveal things to any of our natural senses, He can give us dreams, He can speak to our conscience, He can give us thoughts, He can send angels, or He can just give us a sense of "knowing" something. All of these methods God has used as recorded in scripture to speak to men and women. We have to recognize it when it occurs. And only those who are tuning in to "listen" will discern that God is speaking.

Acting

After we ask God to speak and we listen to what He's saying, we then must act on what He's showing us. Most often this means we should speak, pray, or perform a prophetic act based on what we have heard. For example, the Lord could be showing you something to pray and intercede for. There may be an important situation that God reveals to you which requires time in prayer for that situation to change.

When we receive a message from the Lord, It's important for us to act on what we receive and not delay. It's perfectly fine when you get revelation to ask God what it means, but you don't always get the full understanding of what it means. We have to step out in faith on what we receive, remembering prophecy is for edification, exhortation and comfort. We should always make it a point to minister from the place of God's love and His compassion for others. Love never fails, it always sees things in the right context.

Generally, when we receive a message from the Lord, we also get understanding at that moment on how we are to deliver it. If I am asking God for a prophetic word for a person, and I receive one, then most often I am to speak or write down that word and give it to the person. Just a word of caution here: It's important that we operate in a way that we are leaving the person we are ministering to in a better place than where we found them. Prophecy isn't given to embarrass someone or humiliate them in front of others. If you keep the principles of always operating out of love, seeing people the way Jesus sees them, and realizing that the main purpose of prophecy is to reconcile people to God then you will become an effective minister in this gifting.

5 HOW DOES GOD SPEAK

Can we hear God speak? Yes we can! Why? Because Jesus said so in John 10:27, "*My sheep hear My voice, and I know them, and they follow Me.*"

All of His sheep hear His voice. This is something that we need to settle in our hearts. If we are His sheep, we can hear the voice of our Shepherd. You won't often hear Him speak in an audible voice, but we can all listen to Him in the many ways He speaks.

From the beginning, God revealed Himself as a communicator. He created an environment where He speaks through all He created. In Psalm 19 we learn that *"The heavens declare the glory of God, and the sky above proclaims his handiwork. Day to day it pours out speech, and night to night reveals knowledge."* There is a multitude of truth and messages from the Lord in all He has created. And God himself would show up in the garden of Eden to talk with Adam and Eve. So God wasn't a benevolent, disinterested dictator. He became personally involved in interacting with men and women.

The Bible illustrates that God gives messages to men and women through a variety of different methods, utilizing every avenue of communication humans can uniquely receive. I encourage you to explore the scriptures with this lens in mind and record all the different ways God gives messages to men and women. For this section, Let's categorize the different communication methods God uses to the physical senses, spiritual senses, and through supernatural means.

Physical Senses

Humans have five natural senses: sight, hearing, touch, taste, and smell. Most communication between humans occurs by these five senses. However, these senses can also be used by God to convey His thoughts to us. For example, God had Moses build a tabernacle made out of many different materials. This tabernacle had to be constructed according to God's design, because the design gave a multi-dimensional illustration of several messages God wanted people to understand. God appealed to the sense of sight, smell, hearing, taste, and touch as the priests and people would interact with the tabernacle design and the different elements God commanded to be put into the service of the tabernacle. The tabernacle and its design and daily service spoke about God's design for sanctification, the holiness of God, the requirement of purity, the daily need for fresh life and hearing God, His call to service, the aroma of His beauty, and so many more messages.

In the first chapter of Jeremiah when God began speaking to him, God asked Jeremiah what do you see? And Jeremiah said I see the rod of an almond tree. Jeremiah didn't know what that meant until God told him, but God did initiate the conversation based on what Jeremiah could see. Jesus instructed a Pharisee named Simon by telling him to look at the woman who was washing Jesus's feet with her tears. He started with the physical representation of brokenness and adoration to illustrate to Simon that his heart was hard. And we see in Psalm 19 that God created the physical universe to speak about how big our God is and how powerful he is to hold all things together in order.

One time David was fighting in a battle and he asked the Lord if he should go up to a stronghold of the Philistines. The Lord said to him, when you hear the sound of marching in the trees then go; that is a sign to you that I have given this enemy into your hands (1 Chronicles 14:13-16). In this situation, God spoke through something David would hear with his ears to convey that He was going to give David victory. God also instructed Joshua to walk around Jericho for seven days and blow the trumpet, but not to go into Jericho until the last day. On the last day they were to blow the trumpet several times then give a shout. And when they did, the walls of the city came down. Again, through sound, God spoke and signaled that the city was given to Israel.

One of the interesting facts about the sense of smell is that the human nose can detect at least one trillion distinct scents (study published by the Science journal).[1] And it has been scientifically proven that emotions such as fear, disgust, and memories can be triggered through the sense of smell.[2] We are fearfully and wonderfully made, and magnificently designed to receive messages from our creator. I remember a time when I had just finished a prophetic teaching seminar and I was talking with a friend after this meeting. All the sudden we both smelled birthday candles. There wasn't a birthday celebration around us, no kitchen close by, no food around, nothing that could bring forth that smell. We were in a large building and this was not a manufactured scent. My friend said that day was her birthday. It was God's way of saying happy birthday to my friend. Such a fun revelation! Another time I was ministering in a church meeting, praying for those responding to the message. A woman came up for prayer and as she walked forward, I smelled mentholatum. I asked her if she was wearing mentholatum and she told me no. I explained to her that I use mentholatum to help me breathe better at night when I'm sleeping sometimes, and that's what that specific smell brings to mind. I then asked her if she was having trouble with her breathing, to which she slightly gasped and told me yes. She had been to the doctor several times over the last couple weeks as she was having trouble with her breathing. She was being

---

[1] A team led by Dr. Andreas Keller of Rockefeller University set out to determine the resolution of the human olfactory system by testing how well humans could distinguish mixes of odors. The study was funded in part by NIH's National Center for Advancing Translational Sciences (NCATS). Results were published in *Science* on March 21, 2014. https://www.nih.gov/news-events/nih-research-matters/humans-can-identify-more-1-trillion-smells

[2] The Harvard Gazette, February 27, 2020. https://news.harvard.edu/gazette/story/2020/02/how-scent-emotion-and-memory-are-intertwined-and-exploited/

tested for many different things, but they had not been able to figure out what was wrong. So, with this information, I knew this scent was a word of knowledge that we were to pray for her ability to get her breath and for God to restore her strength. We prayed and the Lord answered with healing in her ability to breathe more deeply.

The Bible speaks about the still, small voice of God. I would classify this as part of the hearing sense although hearing this voice does not really come through our physical ears. Elijah had an encounter when he was running from Jezebel. He went to a small cave on a mountain, after he entered the cave, a strong wind, fire, and an earthquake hit the mountain. The scripture said God was not in any of those natural things. And then, a still small voice began speaking with Elijah, and this voice was God. This passage of scripture doesn't indicate if the voice was internal in Elijah, or if it was registering externally to his ears. But I can suggest to you that God does still speak this way, and this voice comes to us internally. I've heard this voice many times, and it is distinguished by realizing these thoughts were not something I was generating, but rather coming from God. It's important to realize that when God speaks this way, it absolutely never contradicts His nature or His written word.

These illustrations both from the Bible and my own experiences are just a few examples of the many different ways God can use our physical senses to convey His thoughts to us.

Spiritual Senses

I classify the following as spiritual senses; visions, feelings, emotions, and knowing. All of these experiences of God speaking through these senses are found in the scriptures. When we experience them ourselves, they will require our interaction to first recognize their occurrence, and then our acknowledgement that God is conveying a message to us through what we experienced.

The most common way God gives revelation is through visions. I call these quick picture flashes in the mind. Sometimes visions can be longer and more intense, too, such as the time when Peter was on a rooftop in the town of Joppa and he saw a giant sheet come down from heaven with all these animals on it. In Peter's vision, it was like he was transported into the vision itself and he lost awareness of his natural surroundings. Ezekiel had this happen often, as well as Isaiah and Jeremiah.

I first started recognizing God speaking with me through visions that I would get when praying. I remember once when praying for a family member who was being influenced in a negative way by a friend. I was praying for this situation when all of a sudden in my mind a "mini-movie" started playing and I saw this friend and my family member in a room. Then all of the sudden a giant wall came down from above and split the room in two and neither could reach the other. I knew this was an answer to prayer and God was going to separate them. In the next week after praying this, the friend received a notice they were being transferred to another state…and my family member and this person never got together again after that.

The visions you receive as revelation from God aren't controlled by you. This is a distinct difference between what some people practice as "envisioning your success" or picturing yourself accomplishing something. A vision given during interaction with God is distinguished in that it comes to you without you having to dream it up, create it, or control it. Having said this, I want to distinguish between envisioning things and actively engaging in conversation with God regarding any subject matter. I think it is perfectly fine to ask God about specific matters and then allow Him to reveal things to us. In fact, scripture instructs us to ask, seek, and knock and answers will come. The difference is in who controls the answer. When pursuing revelation from God, we allow Him to control the answer.

Once I was praying for some friends who asked me to see if the Lord had a word for them. When I began to pray, all of the sudden I saw a picture of Ronald McDonald's face. I asked the Lord what it meant but at the moment He didn't reveal that to me. So, I simply said to them, "I see Ronald McDonald's face." As soon as I spoke this, and acted in obedience, I knew what it meant. So, I told them both that God was going to give them the "full meal deal". They both started laughing…so I asked them why. They told me that every time they get together, they always pray for one another whenever they have to leave. And, they always say to one another that God is going to give them the full meal deal. Wow! Through that picture of Ronald McDonald's face, the Lord showed me what they would say to each other and confirmed to them that God was going to honor their blessings over each other.

I'm okay if you don't think feelings and emotions belong in the spiritual category. Not every feeling and emotion is given from God, I certainly acknowledge that. But there is plenty of scriptural evidence that God does use feelings and emotions to convey His thoughts. I don't think we should be surprised by that since we were created by Him and He designed us in such a way to be able to interact with Him and the world around us. To gain maturity in understanding, we must have our senses exercised in discernment to distinguish the difference between soulish and spiritual originated messages. This takes time and deliberate pursuit on our part. It is good to be connected with a group of mature believers who can help you grow in this discernment ability.

Let's look at a few scriptural examples to illustrate this method of communication.

In Acts 14 we find a man was healed when Paul had a perception or feeling that the man had faith to be healed.

Acts 14:8-10 (KJV) And there sat a certain man at Lystra, impotent in his feet, being a cripple from his mother's womb, who never had walked: The same heard Paul speak: who steadfastly beholding him, and perceiving that he had faith to be healed, said with a loud voice, Stand upright on thy feet. And he leaped and walked.

The word translated as *'perceive'* is the Greek word *eidō* - and can mean to see or to know something. And this seeing or knowing can occur with the natural sight or by using any of our senses including emotions or feelings.

How did this perception come to Paul? And what did it feel like? The Bible doesn't explain this. The best we can do is compare how you and I perceive things even though we haven't been told anything. We can't explain it, we just know it to be true, especially after It's been reinforced to us over a long period of time that our perceptions can be a reliable source of information to help us make decisions. I'm so glad Paul was bold enough to step out on his perception as this man was healed from a disease he had all of his life. Wow! That happened from just getting a feeling or just a knowing that came to Paul in that moment. From this one example, the Bible illustrates that feelings and perceptions can be extremely spiritual to the point of reversing life-long afflictions.

Let's break this down a little further. Paul perceived the man had faith to be healed, so Paul prompted the man to stand up. What if Paul didn't act on what he perceived? Would the man have been healed? The man had faith, but it wasn't activated until Paul told him to stand. When we prophesy we set in motion events and changes and angels and resources, but all of this is contingent on the response of faith and people acting on it. I am of firm conviction that if Paul had not spoken, the man would have remained in his disease and nothing would have happened. This concept I'm addressing is seen in Genesis chapter 1. Until the word of God is spoken, the world is left formless and void, surrounded by darkness.

Jesus used prophetic perception when a woman touched Him while walking through a crowded street. In Luke 8:43-48 Jesus felt power shift out of Him to someone who touched Him. Amazing! A woman who had a continual hemorrhage for more than a decade was instantly healed.

In Acts 27 Paul perceived that the boat they were traveling aboard was going to take on significant damage, and that their lives would be in danger. He warned the captain; unfortunately, they didn't listen and ultimately the boat was completely lost.

I've personally had a number of encounters where revelation was given to me through perception or feelings. And I venture to say that you have too. Have you ever had an experience where you had a feeling that you needed to pray for a friend or family member even though you hadn't spoken to them about this need at all? And then later you find out that at that exact day you had been praying they were in a situation that was critical and needed God to intervene. God was speaking to you through that feeling so that you would pray on their behalf.

I also have encountered times where God spoke directly through emotions I began feeling when I hadn't been sensing that emotion at all. This isn't unusual or unnatural for God to speak this way. He created the emotions and in fact He himself regularly lives with expressing emotion. And His expression of emotion is perfect, not tainted with any unrighteous expression at all. He is the jealous God who loves you with all His heart. He is the God who sings over His own with fervent joy. He is filled with compassion and love toward His own. Since we were created in His image from the beginning it is only natural that He gives us messages through something we can relate to. Not every emotion you have is a revelation, but there are more times than you probably recognize where it was. Let me put this challenge to you for consideration. The next time you have an emotion which isn't normal for what you typically experience, ask God if He is speaking to you. Or write it down and what was happening and review if this was indeed a revelation you were getting.

The last spiritual sense in which God can give you revelation is through the spirit of knowing. Jesus operated in the spirit of knowledge according to Isaiah 11:2. The bible also identifies for us that Jesus operated in the fullness of the Spirit, without measure. There are several examples in the Gospels when Jesus knew what people were thinking, what they were saying to one another, or what was about to happen. To me this was simply Jesus operating in the gift and spirit of knowledge. So how does this operate, and how do we identify it? When you receive revelation by the spirit of knowledge often the way you can distinguish this method is that you just have a knowing. You just know something without getting a vision, or an emotion, or feeling, or any other indicator.

Operating in the gift of words of knowledge as seen in 1 Corinthians 12:8 is different than operating with the spirit of knowledge. The main difference is we can receive words of knowledge using the different methods of revelation that I speak about in this section. When I operate in the spirit of knowledge, I receive revelation by just knowing something. For example, I was ministering in Costa Rica one year with my mother and father-in-law. Each morning the Lord would give me a "download" of what my parents were going to talk to me about. These topics ranged from ministry questions to business items and everything in between. These revelations just came to me as I prayed and fellowshipped with the Lord each morning. I wasn't asking Him specifically about these topics; the information just came to me. These were important discussions, and the Lord was preparing me beforehand. I couldn't possibly have known what they wanted to talk about unless it was revealed to me by the Holy Spirit. The topics were not discussed beforehand, and natural intuition wouldn't have been enough to figure this out.

Supernatural Communication Methods

For this category, I thought it would be good to separate communication methods received through our senses from those that are unusual and distinct.

In that regard, these unusual and distinct messages we receive are based on encounters with angels, dreams from God, the audible voice of God, encounters with Jesus himself, or any other non-natural communication from God. The distinction in these messages is that they are absolutely unusual, are not in any way able to be controlled by the individual receiving it, and are typically clear in their messaging.

There are several recorded encounters in the Bible where God sent angels to give messages to men. Some that come to mind are the encounters that Abraham, Joshua, Manoah, and Paul had, although there are many others. Before destroying Sodom and Gomorrah, God sent 3 angels to visit Abraham to let him know that these cities would be destroyed and that before the destruction began, they would deliver Lot and his family from the cities. Joshua also encountered an angel before conquering the first city in the promised land. In Joshua 5:13-15 an angel named the Captain of the Lord's host appeared to Joshua with a drawn sword. This was significant because they were just about to siege the city of Jericho and this angel gave Joshua and the Israelites confidence that the Lord was sending his army to help them conquer that city. Manoah and his wife encountered an angel as recorded in Judges 13:3-21 who told them about their son Samson and what he would do and how they should raise him. Paul was visited by an angel on a ship to give him the message that God would spare his life and the life of all on the boat because Paul was to testify before Caesar about who Jesus is.

Dreams and their interpretations are a large subject and there are several excellent books written about this topic. Several times God used dreams to convey messages in the Bible. And He still does this today. Some of the dreams in the Bible provided no room for misinterpretation. In others, the interpretation was absolutely critical to perceive the message God was giving. In either case, the dream itself was not controlled by the person but God was inspiring the dream to provide a distinct message. Joseph, Mary's husband, had two dreams which were absolutely clear as to their meaning as recorded in the books of Matthew, Mark, Luke and John. In one of the dreams an angel appeared to Joseph and told him the name of the boy in Mary (Jesus) and not to be afraid. In another dream, God spoke to Joseph and told him they were to leave the city of Bethlehem and go to Egypt. Joseph, Jacob's son, was a dreamer and God gave him several messages regarding his life and how he would be elevated into a place of ruling. He also was able to interpret dreams that others had which were messages from God, and the recipients of the dreams didn't know their meaning until Joseph helped. Daniel also had the ability to interpret dreams as he did this on a number of occasions for those who were ruling in Babylon. In all of these cases, once the proper interpretation was applied, the messaging was clear and provided critical information regarding God's intentions and events that were to happen in the future.

There are a few instances when the audible voice of God was released as recorded in scripture. As Jesus was being raised from the water following his baptism, the audible voice of God said "This is my beloved son in who I am well pleased!" The voice was heard by Jesus and many of those around the baptism. Another time, when Jesus had just been transfigured before three of the disciples, God's audible voice said "This is my beloved son, hear Him!" What God spoke was not able to be misinterpreted, it was clear. The audible voice of God is still released today on occasion. For example, my wife heard the audible voice of God one night when she had been praying for God to show her who her husband would be. I had never met my wife until that night. I was admitted into the hospital for emergency surgery, and she happened to be my nurse coming out of the surgery. As she left my room from caring for me for the first time, she heard the audible voice of God tell her that I would be her husband. That is the only time she heard the audible voice, but she had no doubt who spoke and what He said. I wouldn't actually know her or meet her until 5 months later when I visited her church, which was on the other side of a very large city in Texas. It was actually a miracle itself that I visited this church. She wouldn't tell me about this incident until after we were married, trusting that God would do what He said without her manipulating circumstances.

Encounters with Jesus himself are extremely rare but they have occurred throughout history and they still happen today. Jesus visited John in a number of encounters while John was on the island of Patmos. It was here that John received the Revelation book of the Bible. Jesus visited Paul on the road to Damascus and challenged Paul to stop persecuting His church. Jesus visited with the apostles before ascending to heaven. So the Bible creates the precedent that this happens. I have heard of a number of encounters Muslims have experienced in the Middle East where Jesus would appear to them in a dream or in a vision experience, and he would reveal to them that he was the Messiah and he was raised from the dead. A number of people who previously followed Islam have turned to Christianity as a result of these Jesus encounters.

Other unusual supernatural encounters in the Bible include Elijah being caught up into heaven from a whirlwind, Philip being transported by the spirit to another city, Enoch entering heaven by translation, Paul going into heaven and receiving messages which he couldn't even put into words, and Ezekiel prophesying to a valley of bones and all of a sudden they became an army of living men. I have heard of many unusual encounters modern day prophets have had regarding angels, translation, appearing in places on the other side of the earth, and more. All of this is in God's realm of communication and shouldn't be considered impossible to Him.

6 INTERPRETATION

Have you ever received a puzzling piece of revelation, yet you knew it was a message from the Lord? Why does He do that? Why doesn't He just speak plainly? We are going to unravel the answers to these questions as we explore the art of interpretation. I call it an art because it requires skill, it doesn't always follow the same pattern, and over time you will grow in this ability as you practice. Interpretation is not a science...there is not an exact formula. There are keys we should become familiar with and we will talk about those in this chapter. But just when you determine a formula, God will switch it up on you because at the end of the day He is more interested in you developing relationship with Him than you discovering another way to get information apart from interacting with Him.

The most practical thing you can do in order to sharpen your skill in interpretation is to become familiar with who God is, how He thinks, and understand His ways. I can't emphasize this enough. Psalm 103:7 says that Moses knew God's ways, and the children of Israel knew His acts. Knowing God's ways is entirely different than knowing what He does. When you dwell in knowing God's ways, you understand the intent of actions and what is mystery to others is plainly understood to you.

Puzzles and Mysteries

God is an excellent communicator. If God wants to speak something very plainly and clearly, He certainly can, and there's been times when He has. So why is it that sometimes his messages are surrounded by puzzles and mysteries? Let's talk about that a little bit.

In Job 33:14-17 it says "For God speaks first time in one way and then a second time in another. Though a person does not perceive it, He'll speak in a dream, a night vision, when deep sleep falls on people as they sleep in their beds, and then He gives them a revelation. He causes a revelation to come to them and He gives them a warning. It's to turn a person from a sin and to cover a person's pride."

There are times when God will speak to us in mystery to turn us away from something that we shouldn't be doing, or he allows that mystery to come to us, to turn us from pride. We get that particular revelation and we can't figure it out, and we realize we're limited and we have to go before the Lord and say, "God, you have to show me. If you don't show me, then I'm not going to know." In that moment, we stop relying on our own ability to understand and we are at the mercy of God to intervene.

When we step into reliance on Him, we acknowledge the fact that we need Him. And in the infinite wisdom of God, He will use mystery to bring us into deeper relationship with Him. In Proverbs 25:2, it says that it's the glory of God to conceal a matter and it's the glory of kings to search it out. This scripture tells us that God allows mystery sometimes so that we would pursue Him, seeking him for the answers. It becomes a benefit to us that we seek Him, search for Him, and try to find out what it is that He's speaking as it draws us closer into relationship and communication with him.

Sometimes God will allow mystery for one particular reason; but other times, at least I've learned through the years, He'll allow mystery because He's doing a multitude of things in our life, through our life, and in the lives of those around us. He could be accomplishing many things just in that one simple act of concealing something in a little bit of mystery.

First of all, He could be drawing us closer to Him. Perhaps we are in a position where we need a deeper and closer relationship with God, and he may say something, or show something to us that we cannot understand without coming to him for the answers. We have to seek him, search his heart, talk with him, engage in communication, and engage in an active pursuit of the scripture to gain understanding in what he wants to reveal to us.

In the middle of our search, what he actually is doing is bringing us closer to him. I think It's so awesome that he allows this, so that through this mystery, we are challenged to find the answers and grow in a deeper level of relationship and involvement with him. As we draw closer to him, we are able to hear his voice with more clarity, it becomes a beautiful and glorious development in our relationship and interactions with God.

Another thing that He could be doing during the middle of allowing mystery is He could be testing our hunger and He can be causing greater hunger. Here's a question for you; how much time and effort and energy are you going to spend in trying to chase and seek and ask in order to hear from Him? If you don't spend much time at all, well, it doesn't seem like you're very hungry to know. He could be testing our hunger, or He could be encouraging us to have an even greater hunger for Him. He could allow some of that mystery to stay in our life because He's trying to grow hunger inside of us to pursue after Him. Along with hunger is what I call passion. He could be increasing passion in us through that same revelation.

God could be drawing us away from the mundane and the routine. A great example I like to think about is when Moses was tending all those sheep, having worked in the wilderness for many years upon fleeing Egypt. The scripture says he'd been there for 40 years. Suddenly, Moses sees a peculiar burning bush on the hill. Although he would have seen burning bushes before in that particular area, because they are common to that area, most of them would have burned for just a few minutes before being consumed, and then the flame would go down and the fire would be gone. But there was this peculiar bush where the fire didn't extinguish and the bush continued to burn. It continued to burn at a high intensity level, not becoming consumed. He probably said to himself, "Well, wait a minute, that's different. That's unusual. I have to search that out. Something is going on here that's not the same."

Moses goes up the mountain to investigate and suddenly, the Lord appears to him in that bush and begins to speak to him. And, Moses' life changed that day. So, there are times when God will allow mystery and things to happen in our life that draw us away from the mundane to introduce a level of excitement; and, lo and behold, all of the sudden the Lord shows up in that moment. These moments are powerful messages from Him and do intriguing things in our life.

It's important for us to be aware when unusual or strange things happen in our life, to pay attention to them. Don't just ignore them. Don't just keep going your own way. Turn aside and investigate. If Moses saw that burning bush and he saw it going like it was even though he saw it wasn't becoming consumed, and he decided, "Well, whatever, I've seen hundreds of burning bushes. Even though that one is still burning, I have other things to do". If he never turned aside to investigate this, he would have never had that encounter. Can you imagine that? Now, I do believe in a God who gives us second chances, so perhaps he would have confronted Moses another way. But it's important for us to turn aside and to investigate, because you never know, God just may be setting you up for a divine encounter.

The last thing I'll mention is mystery requires effort for us to unravel. Once we receive the understanding, we are more likely to hold onto what we've received because we've invested effort. It's the principle that you appreciate what you've worked for as opposed to something just given to you with no investment on your part. God wants us to have an attitude that His words and the things that He reveals to us are precious, that we don't ever count it as a light thing. When God takes time to reveal and to speak from heaven to us, it's an important message that He wants to get across to us, and it should be precious to us. I think there are times when the Lord allows mystery like this to happen because he wants us to have the kind of attitude and a kind of heart that we're going to hold fast to what He says and keep it dear to us and near to our hearts, so that we live, and walk, and operate in that which he reveals.

There are times when the Lord will show up and He'll reveal something to us and we don't quite fully understand it or we don't quite know. Well, If that's not happening in your life, you've got an inferior life. You should have mystery in your life. There should be some experiences or encounters you've had that you don't quite fully understand yet. Just because you don't understand something right away, doesn't mean that it has no value to you. It could be that what has been revealed to you is going to be shown to you many years from the time that you first get it. That's not unusual from a biblical standpoint. For example, many of the prophets wrote about the coming Messiah yet had no idea how or when

He would show up.

For example, in my early 20's, I received a dream right before I graduated from college. For that particular dream, I didn't understand it at the time, and it didn't happen in my life until I was 46 years old. So, the Lord gave me a dream about something that was going to happen in my life twenty-five years in advanced of me understanding what it meant. I asked Him for understanding and revelation about that particular dream for all those years. Now, I don't want to paint a picture that I was doing that every day. I certainly didn't. God had me involved with so many different things, but I do want you to understand that it was something that I asked Him about, talked to Him about, thought about and pondered about for many years, and yet I didn't quite fully understand it until the time in which it actually transpired and took place in my life. That was such a key revelation for me to know that God was with me in that time, and that He had gone before me and showed me that He was going to prepare a place for me in that time and circumstance in my life. It was so important to Him that he showed me 25 years before it happened.

The principle of speaking mystery long before its revealed occurs throughout the scripture. In the history of Israel, there were some words that God gave 400 years in advance of when that particular prophecy was going to take place.

But the Lord had a message, and he wanted it to be understood and he gave it to help the people during the time it would take place, that they'd know, that they'd know, that they'd know that God was in the midst of those moments, and who had spoken to them. So don't ever get frustrated if you have a little bit of mystery; there are so many wonderful things God is accomplishing.

Symbolism

Now Let's explore some different ways to interpret that we can learn from scripture. One of the different ways that we can understand revelation is to first understand that God will often use symbolism. There are biblical symbols, contemporary symbols, and personal symbols that God will show you or reveal to you as you are trying to understand revelation. For example, the cross is a well-known biblical symbol which means a place of suffering and redemption. If you saw a vision of a cross as you're prophesying to somebody, then you can certainly take the biblical meaning of what the cross means, and that would probably fit with what it is that God is trying to reveal to the person that you're ministering to. There are so many biblical symbols it would be a good idea to get familiar with the many symbols in the Bible and to consider their meaning.

Here is a tricky situation. What if God shows you a lion? How will you interpret that? For example, the lion in the Bible could be interpreted as something good or bad. Jesus is known as the Lion of the Tribe of Judah. And there is a scripture that uses the lion as a symbol of Satan…the enemy comes in like a roaring lion seeking whom he may devour. Symbols like this can have dual meaning, so It's essential we ask the Lord to show and emphasize to us which meaning He is emphasizing. The key here is to communicate with the Lord, and then listen for His guidance.

God can use a contemporary symbol. A contemporary symbol is something that has particular meaning to your society and the culture you live in. For example, if you saw the Nike swoosh, you would know what that would mean. It will mean "Just do it." So if you saw that little swoosh symbol, then you know that you're supposed to interpret that as, "Okay, God is saying to you, just do it. Just do what it is that He's saying to do."

Then another way that God will use symbols is that he will use personal symbols. Personal symbols are things that have particular meaning to you but may not mean the same thing to someone else. Let me give you an example of this. Let's say that you saw a picture of a dog as you were prophesying to someone. Now that dog to you is going to mean something different depending on what kind of relationship you have with dogs. If I saw a dog in a vision I would interpret that as being something as friendly, like God is going to give you a good friend, or God is going to cause friends to come to you, or that God wants you to understand that He is your friend. I would interpret it based on friendship because in my life, I've had good experiences with dogs. I think most of my life I've always had a dog as a pet. So, I would look at that as being a friendly symbol. Not everyone has a good experience with dogs. If your experience with dogs was negative, you may be an individual that would definitely think something bad or something wrong is about to happen, and that would be true for you. If God showed you a dog, then that will be a symbol for talking about something difficult or bad, or something evil about to take place. Depending on your understanding of that symbol, that's how God is speaking to you. That's what I mean by personal symbols. These are things that have a particular meaning to you as an individual and you would be able to interpret it and understand what it is that God is saying through that.

    I think it is important to point out that you may not understand what it is you see or sense when prophesying. You may have received a picture of something or a word but you have no context for understanding what that means. There are some times when I've ministered and prophesied with people, that God would say something to me or show me something that I just had no idea what it meant. In fact, I may have never heard of it before. Let me give you an example about one of those particular words. One time I was ministering to a woman at a conference and the Lord said to me, "Lalapalooza." That's what He said. I don't think I've ever used that particular word in a sentence before in my life. I probably heard the word before somewhere but it certainly is not a word that was in my conscience. One of the things that I usually try to do is I usually try to have a smartphone or an iPad with me and when I'm in ministry sessions I'll try to look up things that I get so that I can understand what it is that God is trying to say or show me. So, I had to look that word up, "Lalapalooza." I found out that there was a special music event, I think it happens somewhere in the Michigan or Illinois area, somewhere up there, but they call it a

Lalapalooza. It's a big festival of musicians that get together. So, I understood from that, that God was talking about how He's releasing to this woman the ability to worship and operate in worship in a really creative manner. That's how I prophesied to her. I just prophesied according to the revelation that God gave me. But, you see, if I didn't have a way to look that particular word up, I wouldn't know how to interpret that. I'll use tools like that to help me and I encourage you to consider doing something similar to help you. To finish the story of this unusual word, the woman and her family had created a worship band, so this word was a strong confirmation of God being with them in what they were doing.

The Lord might give you a scripture verse either by bringing the verse to mind or the reference (like John 14:1). It's good to have your Bible with you, so that you can look up scriptures. Whenever I'm ministering, I'll have my Bible with me, my iPad, or my smartphone in order to access the scriptures to help me interpret.

Sometimes as you're ministering to somebody, and you look at them, all of the sudden that person looks like somebody that you know. Well, that could actually be a message from the Lord and a way that he is delivering a message for you to give to them. The person that you know probably has attributes or characteristics that God is highlighting to you for that person you are prophesying to. Or, it could be that the person you know has a particular situation in their life, and the person you are prophesying to is going through something similar. God is using the symbol of another individual that you know and characteristics about them to help you understand how to minister to the person that's standing before you. How do you tell which of the characteristics of the person you know is being highlighted for you to prophesy about? Great question...that's where asking comes in play. If It's not exactly obvious which characteristic God is highlighting to you, then ask God to show that to you. And trust that He will.

Although I won't cover every possibility of what you may encounter regarding symbolism, there is one other I want you to be aware of that I've noticed has been encountered on a fairly frequent basis. There are times when you get a word from the Lord and you're actually seeing the enemy's plans. This can come in the form of something difficult or bad that you see is going to happen or is happening in a person's life. So what I'll do is I will draw on my understanding of what the Bible has to say about this situation and I will prophesy from that position. For example, I knew by revelation that a man was about to be removed from our church because of his disruptive behavior. So I counseled with him about how he can respond and change his behavior. And I encouraged him on what God can accomplish in his life if he would submit to God's plan. I didn't just tell him he was going to be removed...that's easy to do. What is needed more is giving people understanding of what God wants to do in the situation. And that requires knowing God's ways. God didn't show this to me beforehand just to give a warning, but rather to help counsel someone into the path of life. That is glorious ministry and a place we should always work to enter into, especially when we are seeing what the enemy wants to do in a person's life.

Modes of Interpretation

There are different modes of interpretation that you should be aware of. What I mean by this is there are different levels of understanding you will operate in when receiving a prophetic word. For the sake of this discussion, I will refer to receiving of prophetic words as revelation. This will be helpful language to use and is actually more descriptive of what occurs. When the Lord is giving you a prophetic word for someone it comes in a form of revelation. Something is "revealed" to you which is the beginning of a prophetic word that God is showing. God will "reveal" to you a vision, a song, a sense, or some other method of communication (what we covered in the previous section under How Does God Speak). But when this revelation comes, it will come with various levels of understanding.

Sometimes you will get a revelation and know exactly what it means; you have the revelation and the full interpretation. Then there will be times when you get just part of the interpretation with the revelation, and other times all you get is the revelation but you have no idea what it means. I've seen the Lord operate through me and other individuals in these different modes on many different occasions. Don't be discouraged if these different modes happen to you. You 're not broken.

Whenever God gives you revelation , you should always be in a posture of asking him for understanding. Ask, "Lord, I don't know what this means. Will you please show me? Because, God, I need your help. I don't understand it." We can be in that place where we are asking, and He may allow us to linger there for a little bit until He finally reveals it and then we get it. And then we give what we receive.

If you find yourself in the place where all you have is the revelation word but don't know what it means despite asking the Lord several times, I want to encourage you to go ahead and give what you received. It could be that the person you are speaking to will understand everything about it; they'll know exactly how they're supposed to use it, and that will be just enough because they're supposed to provide the interpretation, not you. I've seen this happen on multiple occasions. Once I gave a word to a man and I said to him, "The Lord has a fishing hole for you." I heard this phrase for this man, but I had no idea what it meant and I didn't say anything more than what I heard. Well after I said this, the man's wife and the man started laughing. And they told me later that the husband was currently being invited to go fishing with his cousins in Canada and that he had wanted to do this for many years but never had the opportunity or funds to go. Prior to me giving this word, he was unsure if he should go. The word I gave him was a confirmation that God was in this and was opening the door for him to go.

There are times when God will give you part of a word and only a little bit of understanding. If that happens, act on what you get. Often times God will give you more. I've seen that happen over and over. It's almost like a fishing line where you have a lure on the end of that fishing line and you throw it out. As you throw it out, that lure and the weight of it pulls all the rest of the line out with it. That's what happens when we get a prophetic word sometimes. We'll get a little bit of the understanding, but if we'll just be faithful to operate on what we have, as we throw it out God will add to it and He'll give you more and then you'll be able to give the complete word in the moment.

Filtering and Reflecting

God has uniquely made you and He will use those unique characteristics in the ministry He calls you into. When you prophesy, it is inevitable that you will interpret and filter things through who you are. Because of this, it's so important that we continue to walk with the Lord and allow Him to purge us of things that can get in the way of being a pure vessel. When we hear revelation, when we receive things from the Lord, we're filtering it through our character. We're filtering it through our mind and our emotions and the experiences that we've had. Because of this It's important to be a disciple of Jesus, abiding in the word of God and allowing His word to abide in us.

To be an effective prophetic voice we must spend time knowing Him and knowing the word of God. As we get more and more of the word of God inside of us, we'll be able to understand God better. We'll be able to understand when He says something, even if it is a slight nuance of His heart. When we know our Father, how He thinks and how He operates, we will be much more effective.

I believe 1 Corinthians 13 offers another key aspect of proper interpretation. This chapter is famous for its perspective on the character of love and how it acts, responds, and treats others. Revelations 19 tells us that the spirit of prophesy is the testimony of Jesus. Therefore, it is only natural to say that the pure prophetic spirit will agree with the one whose name is Love. In that regard, I encourage you to step into the nature of love as described in 1 Corinthians 13. As you do, you'll see people differently, you'll have a better perspective on how God sees them, and in turn you'll be better equipped to minister to the depths of people's hearts.

7 PROPHETIC PROTOCOLS

There are several principles in the scripture to help guide us in becoming impactful prophetic ministers. This chapter will focus on some of those principles, or what I call protocols.

One of the things that we need to remember is that the main goal in prophesying is to convey the Lord's heart in bringing edification, encouragement, and exhortation to the person we're ministering to. That's basically what the Holy Spirit was teaching us through Paul in 1 Corinthians 14. And we want to make sure that at the end of the day, the person is left in a better place than when we began to minister to them. We're prophesying to help bring people into an encounter with the Lord that they have not yet experienced. Our ministry should result in leaving them in a better place. We should leave them in a place where they are moving towards God in their relationship.

This brings me to the first protocol that I'd like to share with you. The scripture tells us that God is love. When we are ministering in the prophetic, we want to make sure that we're lining up with what the scripture teaches in 1 Corinthians 13, that love is not thinking of its own. Love always thinks well of its object. Love is always kind. Love is always pure. Love operates in an excellent way. And that's the first protocol which is to minister out of the spirit of love, which is the testimony of who our God is.

God wants to bless. God wants to redeem. God's heart is to draw people to Himself. And that should be our impact. We should be causing people to move closer to the Lord. And there's nothing that causes people to move closer to someone else than the spirit of love. Love attracts, fear and judgment repel. People will embrace love. We want to make sure that we're operating out of that spirit so that the individual that we're ministering to embraces the Lord. They're embracing Him in new encounter. They're embracing Him with fresh desire. They're embracing Him with enlivened passion that causes them to move into the next realm of destiny that God is calling them into.

Now, if you are ever in a place where you're ministering prophetically and you feel like you are out of energy and the ability to hear, turn to love. When I turn to love, I normally am able to see people in a whole different way. I'm able to view them from God's heart and God's perspective when I operate out of love.

When I begin to think that way, the Lord normally gives me fresh strength. So, when I turn to love, I receive new inspiration. When I turn to love, I am able to see beyond what I was seeing with my natural eyes and I am able to begin seeing with God's eyes. That gives me fresh strength for the moment and it helps propel me beyond my own natural limitation.

God wants it to become part of our character, that we would be like Him in how we minister. When I turn to love, I am actually embracing him in a place of brokenness and weakness in my own heart. And God begins to fill my void with Himself. In these moments, I am actually being conformed into the image of Christ. Isn't that cool? We have the opportunity to do that in prophetic ministry. We can be conformed to the image of Christ in the moments we're ministering. I find that very thrilling because in that I receive a blessing. My blessing is to become like Him. And as you turn to love, you'll find that your ministry will be highly empowered. In fact, it will take you into places and realms that you've never known existed. It's a new adventure that the Lord is calling you to.

We want the brightness of Jesus to come down and minister into us as we're gazing at Him in the prophetic. When we prophesy, we're peering with intensity and anticipation into His glory, which sometimes is so bright, it's difficult to keep our spiritual eyes open. But you know what? That's what we need to do. We need to let the son of God shine into our hearts, shine into our vision, to cause us to have glimpses of Him that go beyond the natural.

It's important that when we prophesy that we are prophesying in a safe place. Let me use this scripture to give context to that statement, prophesying in a safe place. In 1 Corinthians 14:29, the scripture tells us to let the prophets speak two or three and let the other judge. In other words, let's be sure that when we minister, we're ministering in a place where there's two or three witnesses, so there is more than just you and the person that you're prophesying to. That's what I refer to as prophesying in a safe place.

It's safe for the person who's being ministered to that there are other witnesses that are hearing it and it's actually safe for you too, as a prophetic minister. If you are prophesying to someone secretly, just between you and them, what could happen is they'll take your words and they'll twist them and use it against you to judge and criticize. I've seen this happen before where someone would think they heard something that a minister prophesied, but it wasn't correct. It was taken out of context or it was what that person wanted to think that the minister prophesied, but it really wasn't what they said.

To be in a safe place, you want to prophesy where two or three witnesses hear so that every word is established. In fact, 2 Corinthians 13:1 says, "In the mouth of two or three witnesses shall every word be established." Because of this, you want to avoid backroom prophecies; prophecies that happen in the street or in the parking lot where it's just you and that other person. If you can I would avoid that. It's not healthy for you. It's not healthy for the person receiving that word, and it also helps to make sure that every word is established when there's more involved than just you and that person. This protocol is not a rule, but a safeguard to follow when possible.

We should be careful to not despise prophesying, but instead prove all things and hold fast to that which is excellent. That's 1 Thessalonians 5:20-21. In this scripture we see there is a principle that tells us to test and prove every word. Just because someone prophesied to you or tells you, "Thus sayeth the Lord" doesn't mean that it was from God. It could be that the person who was speaking was submitting to a wrong spirit. They could be projecting their own thoughts and feelings on you instead of what God is saying. It could be that when they received a revelation, they misinterpreted that word or that revelation. Because of this, we are to test and judge every prophetic word, and encourage others to test and take any words you give before the Lord, too.

Here's another important protocol to remember. It's important for us to remain teachable. The best way that I can illustrate this is when I first began to prophesy the way I would receive revelations was though a dream or through what I call a vision. The visions I would usually receive were like mental pictures, and I knew it was from the Lord. I don't know exactly how I can tell you that I knew it was from the Lord other than I just knew and over time God proved Himself to me over and over. I would prophesy according to the picture or according to the dream that God gave. That's how I functioned for a number of years. In the past 15 years, the Lord has opened my understanding and experience to several new ways that He speaks. If I didn't have a teachable spirit, I would have disregarded these other ways God speaks.

The other aspect of being teachable, is that although I am ministering, I am also in the place of learning. God wants to impart wisdom, give us glimpses of His heart, and reveal secret things to us all during the time we are ministering to others. It's a wonderful way to live, and a thrilling adventure to walk with God in this ministry.

In the past nine or so years, I've begun to get things like walking into a room and just having a knowing. I didn't see a picture.

I didn't get any dreams. I didn't get an encounter, physical touch, or anything like that. But when I walked into the room, I just had a knowing. This is what's referred to in Isaiah chapter 11 where it says that one of the spirits that is on Jesus is the spirit of knowledge. That knowingness just came into me. And of course, I operated in that and prophesied from it. It was true. God confirmed. Be willing to learn from God because He's going to have new encounters for you, and new ways for you to express His heart to others. It may not be what you have experienced before.

Another protocol is there are times when we hold onto a revelation we've been given instead of sharing it. There are some words that we pray into and there's some words that we say, and it's important for us to know the distinction. We have to develop this discernment over time as we walk with the Lord. Sometimes the Lord gives you revelation to pray and intercede about. If you were to speak what you received it could actually cause harm. It could actually cause the situation that you are going to speak into to not have grace or peace to change. Why did God show you? Because He is inviting you into interceding on behalf of that person so that grace would be released for this person to step into freedom. God wants to engage us as His bride and as co-partners to see things shift in the earth and to bring the Kingdom of Heaven into the earth. He will allow us to see things ahead of time of what He wants to do. He's inviting you into a position to pray into the situation, and to partner with Him, watching His desires for that situation come to pass.

When prophesying to somebody, make sure that they are willing for you to prophesy to them. For example, if you are in a church and you get a word for a person who is sitting several seats away from you, don't just walk right up to them and say, "Thus sayeth the Lord…" That's normally not a good idea. You don't know if they're ready to hear anything. You don't have their permission yet to speak into their life. Before ministering, you should ask if they would like to receive a word from you. This is how I do it. Over the years I've learned that when I receive a word for somebody, I'll go up to them and tell them my name first and then normally say something like, "I'm always praying and I'm asking God to show me things for other people. And as I was thinking about you, I felt like I was getting an impression that I believe is for you. Would you mind me sharing that with you?"

If you'll approach them right, usually what they'll tell you is, "Well, of course, yes. I'd love to hear that." If they are resistant to it, then that's okay. You just move on. Maybe what you do with that word is you write it out. There might be another time they come back to you and say, "Yeah, you know what you were going to share with me? I'd like to hear it now." And so you could share it then. If you never get the opportunity to speak that word, you could just pray for them about that particular word.

I've found that sometimes people want to know who you are before you give them a word. In that case, what I do is tell them a little bit about who I am, where I fellowship, and a bit about my relationship with God. That is usually the type of information people want to know before giving them a word. I think those are safe topics to discuss and certainly don't be offended if someone asks you things like that. It's a good protocol to have on both sides that when we're prophesying to people, we should let them know who we are. It makes for a safe environment for the giver and receiver.

Here's another important protocol to remember; does the prophecy bear witness to the scripture? If it's a true word from the Lord, it's not going to disagree with principles in the scripture. Let me give you an example. There have been a number of pastors I've heard discuss this and testify about this, where they had someone come up to them during a meeting and would say something about their marriage. "You're actually not supposed to be married to the person that you're married to. You're supposed to divorce them, and you're supposed to marry so and so." That's a great example of something that's totally against God's word. That's not God, that's not his spirit, and God doesn't speak that way. The person prophesying this way is obviously being moved by a spirit of lust or deception. Unfortunately, this example actually happened and the person got a divorce and did what was prophesied to them. In both cases where I've seen this happen, it resulted in a horrible church split with several lives pushed into ruin. So, the bottom-line principle is to test every revelation we receive with the word of God before speaking this to others. God does not contradict His word and His character.

The last protocol is that we know in part and we prophesy in part. When prophesying we only get part of the full counsel of God. There are times when God will give me a fuller amount of detail about the picture or the place where God is bringing that person into. But even then, I'm only getting part of the whole counsel of God. Just be mindful that, whatever piece that God gives us, we should just go with that piece because that's what the Lord wants to speak through us into that person's life. If we'll just be faithful to operate in the piece He gives us, God can take that and then shift this person into getting the rest of the revelation that God wants to reveal to them. You and I should focus on the part we get and let God bring the rest in His sovereignty.

One other thing to consider; I always encourage people who are ministering in the prophetic to minister in teams. I encourage this as it goes back to the principle that when we prophesy, we know in part and we prophesy in part. I encourage you to minister in teams because there will be something that you receive that another person from your team can be prompted to pick up on. And then, the person you're ministering to will receive a fuller picture of revelation. And then sometimes, the third person will pick up on something else and they'll be able to add fuller meaning to the prophetic encounter. This releases a fuller picture during team ministry. But again, even then, we're still just ministering in part because we are only showing or shedding light on that particular issue in the person's life. God has so many more things to say to them and share with them as He invites them into encounter with Him.

At the end of the day, when we're ministering, we want to make sure that we're building people up, edifying them, causing grace and the comfort of God to enter into their heart. They should walk away knowing they have encountered the Lord, and that God brought them to a place where they're being drawn into His presence. If we can minister in that way, then we've had a successful prophetic session.

8 CONTENDING FOR WORDS

How can we make sure that we live, walk, and operate in all that God has called us to? Over the years I've watched people receive prophetic words, and I've noticed that some people don't ever live out what God declared to them. I think there can be many reasons why this happens. This chapter will focus on a few key principles that we have to embrace to live in the fullness of what God has declared to us. I've learned over the years that there's effort required on our part to lay hold of prophetic words.

Choosing to Agree and Pursue

For some people in the body of Christ it seems like they have an attitude of, "Well if it was from God it's going to happen and there's nothing I can do about it, it's just going to have to all fall in place and it's all on God to do that". I don't believe that's a right way to approach prophecy. I don't believe it is true that if you get a prophetic word, revelation, or dream that there's no effort required on your part to live in that declaration. In actuality, there are things that you and I have to do to embrace the word. We don't want God to give us revelation or speak a prophetic word to us and then let it fall to the ground and have nothing to do with it. There is choice that's required on our part and we must decide what we're going to do with those prophetic declarations.

Let me give you an example. God gave Samuel a revelation for King Saul. And in this revelation God said to Samuel, "Samuel, I want you to give instruction to Saul that he's to go and kill the Amalekites, wipe all of them out including their king, and all of their sheep and their cattle. Don't leave anything living on their land because of what they have done as a people and the way that they have shown disgrace towards my people" (see 1 Samuel 15). God's judgment was upon them. King Saul was the one who was supposed to carry out God's judgment. So, in obedience, Samuel went to Saul and he told him this word. Well, if you know the story, Saul decided that he wasn't going to kill all of the Amalekites. In fact, he spared the king and he also allowed the people to keep some of the sheep and some of the cattle in order for them to have a feast.

Then God said to Samuel, "Samuel go down and tell Saul that he has not followed me fully, he has not obeyed the word of the Lord. He's not fulfilled all of my heart of what I've declared should be done. Therefore, I'm going to take away from him the kingdom where he has been made a king and ruler over Israel." Samuel went down and he told Saul and that day God decided to anoint somebody else to be king in Saul's place because he did not follow all that was in God's heart. Saul was given an opportunity to choose. What was he going to do with that word? Was he going to follow it wholly or was he going to do something else? Because of Saul's choice, that word which was from God wasn't fulfilled through Saul. Unfortunately, the matter doesn't end there. As a consequence of disobedience, Saul was set on a course for losing the kingship of Israel. Not only would Saul not be king in the future, but his entire bloodline was removed from being part of the kingship.

There is choice involved on our part. When we receive a word from God sometimes it'll come in commandment form, and sometimes it will come in a 'here's what the Lord is going to do' or 'here's what He's declared over you' form. There's still choice on our part. We must decide. Are we going to agree with what God says? Are we going to follow and enact what He's called us to do? Are we going to allow things to change and adjust in our lives so that we can line up and agree with what God said and has spoken over us? Usually, to fulfill our part of bringing His words to pass in our lives, there are actions we need to take.

Open Invitation

Let's explore some principles you can find in the scripture regarding our response to prophetic declarations, dreams, impressions, and visions God gives you regarding your destiny and who you're called to be. <u>The first principle is that when you receive a word you've</u>

<u>also received an open invitation to enter into a process to bring to pass the future state that God declared</u>.

When you receive a prophetic word, you have received an invitation from God to enter into adjustment and change in your life to help you obtain that word. There are some things that have to be reconfigured perhaps in your soul, or your circumstances, that will help you become what it is that God declared.

A great example of this principle would be King David. David was anointed to be the king over Israel when he was still a teenager. And, if you read through the scripture, you find out that David didn't become a king until he was in his thirties. It was almost 20 years later when he actually became the king. Why did God tell him so early? What was going on in between? During this interim period there was testing, change, and adjustment happening. When David received the revelation, he had heard the call to kingship but he had to grow in maturity to live in the call. God used the interim period to shape David's soul so that he could be an effective leader for the nation of Israel.

In 2 Samuel 22:31 it says this, "As for God his way is perfect. The word of the Lord is tried and he is a buckler to all those that trust in him." This verse states that the word of the Lord is tried or in another word tested. There's a testing time. In Psalm 105 there's a similar scripture that talks about this testing, it's in verse 17 through 19, and it talks about Joseph. And it says that, "He sent a man before them even Joseph who was sold for a servant whose feet they hurt with iron until the time that his word came, the word of the Lord tried him". Now, that's an unusual phrase; "…until the time that his word came the word of the Lord tried him." In the New Living translation it says, "until the time came to fulfill his dreams, the Lord tested Joseph's character". In the Interlinear Bible it says this, "until the time came that his word, the spoken word of the Lord tried".

Let's look at some of those different key words in these verses to understand their meaning. "Until the time came that his word…". The word *time* means appointed time. It also means circumstance, period, or season. There is a right season when the word is to come to pass. There's an appointed time, there's a season, there's a circumstance that God creates in our life where we're to step in and then that word becomes alive. Everything that God said to us about that season, that's when it all comes to fruition; it comes to pass. Going back to David, God declared to David, "David you're going to be the king". He said that to him when he was about 16 or 17 years old but it wasn't until he was 37 or so that the word came to pass; the appointed time arrived that he would be that which God declared. There's an appointed time. There's a season or circumstances that God is going to bring together where you and I step in to that which He declared.

The next phrase for us to break down is "the word of the Lord tried him". The word tried means to smelt, or refine, or test. There's a testing time for the word, a time when it's being refined, it's being purified, it's being put together. In other words, there's a trying, or a testing, or a purification that takes place. The word of the Lord tried Joseph. How was the word of God trying Joseph?

Joseph received dreams about his life and how he was going to be a ruler, even over his own house, and his mom, and his dad, and all of his brothers. He received these dreams when he was a young man. And, the entire time Joseph spent unjustly in prison, those dreams kept coming back to him, and they tested him. What was being tested? His heart was being tested about the strength of his faith. Would he believe what God declared, or would he lose faith? You have to wonder what his thoughts were during those many days and weeks and months of living and serving others in prison. Joseph was in the prison at least 10 to 15 years, because he was likely a teenager or in his early 20's when he was imprisoned, and he was in his 30's when he finally got released from prison. During the time he was in Pharaoh's dungeon serving, he probably was tempted to believe these dreams were wrong because his circumstances vastly contradicted these dreams; here he was living in a prison in a foreign land, he was far from being in a place of rulership. The word tested him. And, he had a choice; "am I going to believe?"

Until the season when the word of God is supposed to take place in our life there's a testing that happens in our hearts. The testing is 'are we going to believe"? Are we going to have faith and agree that what we heard from God, God is able to bring to pass, and he's able to cause it to take place?

Remaining in a place of believing God's report is critical. Because without faith, it's impossible to please

God (Hebrews 11:6). It's also critical, as we will likely not recognize the hour of change God brings to open the door for that prophetic word to come to pass. Stepping out of believing desensitizes us to the moves of God around us.

Here's another testing that you're probably all familiar with - Abraham. His name was initially Abram. And, when God said to him, "your name is no longer Abram but it's Abraham, father of many", that in itself was a test to him hearing that new name and It's meaning as it seemed to contradict his circumstances. Would he believe God was able, and that God was going to bring this promise to pass? The word of the Lord tried him. The word of the Lord was testing him. He had to learn to agree with God even though all of his circumstances, and all of his situations were telling him the total opposite.

Joseph had to speak to his soul. There was a wrestling that was occurring deep within him - the wrestling that occurs in every man and woman's soul that hears God's word over their lives. Whose report shall you believe? I imagine Joseph's conversation was something like this, "God you said I would be a ruler. I don't rule anything. I'm just cleaning up after men. I'm feeding them. I'm just serving them. I'm a servant. How am I ever going to be a ruler?" During the test, he could allow doubt to come into his mind. And of course, who wouldn't agree with Joseph if he did enter into doubt? But the fact is, he continued to believe. He continued to trust God. "I don't know how you're going to do it God, but I know that's what you said to me. That's what you showed me in a dream."

The same thing happened with David. He found himself running around in the wilderness, taking shelter in cave after cave. Saul was chasing him everywhere, and he thought he was going to die. He ended up retreating to the land of the Philistines to escape from Saul because he thought, "If I stay here in Israel he's going to kill me. How am I ever going to be a king? I don't know. I'll probably die in the wilderness." His situation was so far from God's promise, that in human thinking and logic, it would have seemed impossible. We read David's struggle throughout the book of Psalms when David frequently has doubts, but then he makes a conscious shift, and repositions his thinking and his heart to belief and trust in God.

Until the season arrives when the word of the Lord is supposed to take place, bear fruit, and become reality, there's a testing that happens. During this phase our character is being refined, our faith is being refined, and God is helping us become what we need to become so that we are able to operate and be all that God has called us to be. If we stay in faith and pursuit of God, a refining occurs in our character, helping us be successful and fruitful in the particular calling He's placed over our lives.

During the trying time, Joseph's character was changed, which brings me to this thought. There are parts of us that look like Jesus, they act like Jesus, and that's good. And then, there are parts of us that really need adjustment. There may be parts of us that when somebody says a disagreeable word to us, or something happens, we lose patience. It's in this type of moment that we see a need for God to refine our character. This refinement is essential, and perhaps more valuable than getting to the end goal of fulfilling a prophecy. This is the part where God is conforming us into the image of His dear son (Romans 8:29). It is likely that this adjustment and change process that we go through is essential to our success, as that part of our character could become a hindrance to us in being able to operate in what God has called us to be.

Here is an example that illustrates this necessary growth process from the Bible. God called Moses to lead Israel out of the land of bondage, out of Egypt into the promised land. But there came a day where God said to Moses, "Moses, I want you to speak to the rock and then water's going to come forth from it and that'll be able to give a drink to all of the people, and the cattle." And Moses got irritated from what happened by all of the complaining, and the bitterness, and the back talking, and everything that was happening among the leaders and so he got angry. In his anger, he struck the rock and the water came out. And, God said to Moses, "Because you didn't exemplify me before the people, you're not going to be able to lead them into the promised land" (see Numbers 20:10-13). It was very important for Moses to reflect God at that point in time because there was a lesson that God was trying to teach Israel through him speaking to the rock instead of striking the rock. Because of Moses actions, he wasn't able to fulfill what it was that God wanted him to fulfill to be a testimony to Israel.

There are parts of our character that need to be refined

so that we don't make mistakes like Moses made. Or, it could be that we have a character flaw that will prohibit what God wants to do in us and through us in the time where we enter into that word or that calling that God has on us. The refining time is our preparation before we can inherit the promise.

There are many different parts of your character and my character that God wants to shine through. He wants us to reflect the glory of God. Every man and every woman are called to reflect his likeness. Because of this, we have many identities in which we are supposed to be a reflection or a likeness of Jesus. For instance, here's just an example of a few things that I've been called to be. I'm a father as I am blessed with four daughters. I have a beautiful wife so I'm also a husband. I'm a son. I'm a bank examiner. I'm a prophetic captain. I'm a missionary. I'm an evangelist. I am a man. I am a leader. I'm a child of God. I am part of the body of Christ. I am part of the bride of Christ. I am a voice.

In all of those different identities I have, I've been called to reflect Jesus. Because of this, there's a refinement of character that has to take place in every one of those aspects so that I can be like Christ and honor God in my life.

Some of these identities I walk in with great effectiveness, and in some of these identities I'm still learning how to be like Jesus. I possess varying levels of God's likeness in these identities but I haven't fully occupied all that God has called me to. So, I'm in the process of laying hold of the calling that God has on my life. Now, let's consider some of those prophetic words or those declarations that God has said to you. What aspect of a word or destiny that God's called you too can you say that you have completely fulfilled, and reflect Christ at this point in time? If there are aspects or destiny that you can identify that you haven't fully embraced, then there's likely a process you're still going through, during which God is refining your character, so that you can step into the fullness of what you are called to be. God gives many provisions to help us possess what it is that He's called us to possess in the middle of this process.

For instance, sometimes God will create a problem to overcome so that we can enter into and become part of the character that we need to become. For example, Joseph needed to learn to be a leader before he could fulfill the dreams God gave him. But before becoming a leader, he had to learn how to put other's interests above his own. So, the Lord allowed Joseph to have a problem to help him learn how to be a leader. He was put in prison, and it was there that he learned how to serve others. This was a valuable lesson for him especially because of the leadership role he would have later in life. Joseph would be responsible for feeding nations through his leadership, and this God-given calling required him to be an effective servant-leader to be successful.

God doesn't always use negative circumstances to shape our lives. For example, He gives us friends to encourage us, helps us to be successful in things we are doing, and provides for us in a thousand different ways. I'm so thankful for people who love me, and care about me, and that speak encouragement to me because it helps me continue to step into faith in this journey that I'm on, to possess and become all that God's called me to be. God can give you a mentor, someone who has gone there and been there before. In fact, I would encourage you to seek out mentors especially in the fields you have been called to.

God can give you a wilderness, a place where it doesn't matter what you do, it doesn't seem like you make progress. What do we learn in the wilderness? We learn how to lean on Jesus. We learn how to trust Him. We learn that there's nothing that can really get us from point A to point B, and we have to trust in Jesus and not our own capability. And by doing this, then we learn how to become intimate with God. Listen, a wilderness can be a blessing and it's not always a curse.

It says in 1 Peter 1:7 that the trial of our faith is much more precious than gold. Because when our faith is made pure there's such a glory that's added to our lives in allowing God to purify us. So, that's principle number one. God invites us into a process so that we might become that future state of what he's called us to. And the important aspect of this particular principle is we must have faith, we must believe, we must continue to look to God and trust him because we know that He is faithful in whatever He has called us to.

Dialoging with God

Here is the second principle that I'd like to touch on.

<u>We need to enter into a dialogue with the Lord regarding what he has declared</u>. This dialogue should include prayer, it should include talking things over with God, discussing with God, it should involve confessing our agreement with what God has said, and sometimes it may need to look like repentance.

When you receive a prophetic word that you believe was from the Lord, you should begin a dialogue with God about that word. That will look like prayer, asking God questions, and many times just taking time to think about what has been said to you. As you're in that place of holy communion with Him, the Holy Spirit will begin to speak to you, to show you, and reveal things to you about this word. As we engage in conversation with God, God begins to reveal more and more to us about what the fulfillment of this word will looks like.

Here's another key point about prophecy. When you and I receive prophetic words, we receive part of the destiny we are called to. It's important for us to enter into a dialogue with God to talk to Him about what this looks like, because there are additional downloads that He wants to give us to help paint a fuller picture of what He's called us into. Unless you keep asking, pressing in, and talking to Him, you will be missing some key details about that revelation that God will show you over time.

God doesn't always show us the whole aspect of a revelation at one time. Part of the reason this occurs is that He is trying to draw us into a process of growing in intimacy with Him. It's not just about you and I getting a word, or a dream, or a declaration and becoming something or doing something. He's inviting you into a relationship with Him where He wants to reveal more of Himself to you. He wants you to discover who He is, and to cause a sense of wonder and awe and impartation of Himself to you during your season of searching out what He is calling you to. You see this is all about relationship. And through mystery, He's inviting us into a place of greater intimacy and closeness with Him.

So, we need to learn to dialogue and talk to Him as you would talk with a friend about what it is that He's said to you, because there's more that He wants to say. Now, let me show you a picture of this in the scripture from Daniel chapter nine.

Daniel was reading through what scripture he had available to him, and in it he found a passage in the book of Jeremiah when God had declared that there was an appointed time for Israel to be taken into captivity and it was going to last for 70 years. And after 70 years, God was going to bring Israel back into the promised land. Daniel learned through reading the scripture that this was something God had promised and was going to do.

Daniel had a choice after reading this passage in Jeremiah. What was he going to do with that knowledge? He could have simply said, "Well that's interesting. I'm just going to sit here and look down from my window to see God do what he promised. It's been about 70 years now, I guess he's going to start moving anytime." He could have taken that attitude and approach. That's not what he did. I'm glad Daniel did what he did. Daniel took that revelation and used it to motivate himself to begin to talk and discuss this with God, and pray to God and repent on behalf of Israel.

I believe God positioned Daniel in that place to be a strategic intercessor for Israel, so that they might inherit the fullness of what God had declared. Because without a Daniel there contending for Israel, praying for this to come to pass, and interceding, perhaps that word would never have come to pass. Think about that. What if Daniel never entered in to pressing in and seeking the Lord? There may never have been a return back to the promised land, even though God declared that's what he wanted to do.

Let's look at what Daniel did when he began to talk to the Lord. "In the first year of Darius, son of Xerxes, who was of Median descent and who had been appointed king over the Babylonian empire. In the first year of his reign, I, Daniel came to understand from the sacred books that according to the word of the Lord disclosed to the prophet Jeremiah the years for fulfilling of the desolation of Jerusalem were 70 in number." Here he came to that revelation as he was studying the scripture. And then, look at what he did. "So, I turned my attention to the Lord and I began to have a strong cry. By prayer and request, with fasting, and with sackcloth and with ashes. And I prayed to the Lord my God confessing in this way. 'Oh Lord God, great and awesome God who is faithful to his covenant with those who love him and keep his commandments we have sinned. We have done what's wrong and wicked. We have rebelled by turning away from your commandments and your standard. We didn't pay attention to your servants the prophets who spoke by your authority to our kings, and our leaders, and our ancestors, and to all of the inhabitants of the land as well."

Wait a minute, hold on. Is this Daniel that we're talking about here? Because as far as what I know Daniel was a righteous man. He wasn't the one who was sinning. He was the one who was faithful. But what did he do? As an intercessor he chose to identify with the people of Israel, and he prayed, and he cried out on their behalf taking their place before the Lord and crying and pouring out his heart to God and asking God, "Would you have mercy? Would you forgive us?" And he began to repent on their behalf. There may be some repentance that you need to do while you are contending for the words that God has spoken to you.

I encourage you to consider stepping into repentance if there are words that you've not seen fulfilled in your life, and that you have neglected. Maybe you have been lazy in your response, or not really taken them seriously. You may have just put them on a shelf and said something like, "Well if it's God I guess he's going to have bring it to pass". But consider what Daniel did. He studied, he learned, he became familiar with what God said, and then he began to seek God and cry out to God, and repent, and ask God, "Will you do something? Will you please have mercy? Will you forgive us for how we've been neglectful?" And then we read that the Lord sends an angel to Daniel and says, "Daniel I've heard your prayer, and I'm going to bring to pass that with which you have been praying and crying out to me about". Remember God's promise, 'When you seek me, you will find me

when you search for me with your whole heart'
(Jeremiah 29:13).

I wanted you to see this picture of Daniel contending in prayer and earnestly seeking God for the fulfillment of his promise, so you will be encouraged to enter into dialogue with God about what He's declared to you. We need to dust off those words, we need to remember those visions, we need to think on those dreams, we need to refresh those impressions and the things that so impacted us. And we need to take them and get into the place of intimacy with God, and begin dialoguing with him and talking to him about those things. And as you do this, you're going to find there will be invitations into relationship, and greater revelation will be given to you. God will show you more about what He declared to you and perhaps He will unveil some key things that need to happen in your life. You will see a shift occur in your spirit and ultimately in your circumstances to bring to pass what He declared.

Embrace what He Confirms

The third principle is that we must embrace what God has confirmed. The biblical example I want to use to explain this principle is the example of Saul. Saul was prophesied to that he was to be the king of Israel. Samuel prophesied this. When Saul was searching for his father's donkeys and he ended up not finding the donkeys, he decided to go to Samuel's house to inquire of him as a prophet where his dad's donkeys might be found. And before Saul even reached Samuel's house,

God had already spoken to Samuel the day before Saul arrived that a young man will come to his house, he's going to be looking for donkeys; and, this is the young man that will be the first king of Israel.

God told Samuel about Saul before he got there, and sure enough the very next day Saul shows up. He was the exact description of what God said that he was going to be. And so then, Samuel anointed Saul that day he arrived. Before Saul left, Samuel told Saul about all of the things that were going to happen to Saul that day as he was going back to his father's house. He told him about how he was going to go walk along this mountain, he was going to run into these three guys, and then some of them are going to have some bread. And then, the next thing that's going to happen is you're going to run into a company of prophets and the spirit of the Lord is going to come upon you. And you're going to begin to prophesy, and at that moment you're going to become another man.

And then, he said to him, and when that happens do whatever's in your heart because the Lord is with you.

It happened to Saul according to everything Samuel said. It's very interesting what happened next with Saul. After all these events occurred, confirming to Saul what Samuel had said, the next thing you read is that he returns to his father's house, and his uncle comes to him and says to him, "So I hear you ran into Samuel?" And he said, "Yes". The uncle asks, "Tell me what he told you". Saul doesn't tell him anything about him being anointed to be a king. He tells him nothing. He kind of acted like nothing had even happened. In fact, the next scene you see is that Samuel calls Israel to a feast, and Saul was supposed to be there, too. And Saul knew that he was supposed to be there, and that Samuel was going to introduce him as the anointed to be the king of Israel, and they couldn't find him. Where was Saul? Saul was hiding among stuff. He was hidden among a bunch of baggage, blankets, and pillows, and all kinds of different supplies. He was hiding himself. In other words, he wasn't embracing the identity he was called to, and he wasn't embracing what God had declared, and confirmed.

We have to step out of the old and we have to step into the new. In other words, if there's something that God has said that you're going to be and he's confirmed it, then you have to choose to step into it. We need to embrace it. We can't hold back. Staying with the old thing means we've rejected the new thing God has called us to. And especially when God not only says it to us, but then he confirms it to us. I mean that's almost like a double stamp of God saying, Hey, I'm upon this word, and I'm with you. And whatever it is that I have declared and said to you, I'm going to be behind it.

We don't want to be like Saul who just halfheartedly walked in the words of God. We need to embrace fully what God declares so that we can become everything that He's said to us and that we might agree with Him and follow Him with all of our heart.

9 TESTED IN THE PROPHETIC

We can be extremely gifted to the point of hearing accurately from God and yet totally blow it when put in the place of giving the revelation. Let's explore two uniquely prophetic men to illustrate character and giftedness. Daniel had giftedness and godly character. Jonah had giftedness, but lacked a portion of God's character.

Once God got Jonah in the place to deliver the message, courtesy of his unconventional ride to Nineveh, he only spoke the judgment that he heard, and he provided no explanation regarding the potential for repentance and how the judgment could be lifted. In fact, after Jonah told Nineveh that God would judge them, he left town and found a cozy spot on the hillside so he could watch the city suffer under God's wrath.

Let's contrast Jonah's behavior with the interaction between Daniel and Nebuchadnezzar. God gave Nebuchadnezzar a dream that basically showed that the king was going to be judged because of the pride in his heart. After Daniel heard the dream, he gave the interpretation of what it meant to Nebuchadnezzar. If Daniel had the same heart attitude as Jonah, he wouldn't have explained anything further to the king. But Daniel's heart was different. He gave counsel to the king on how the king could prolong his tranquility. He told the king that if he would do what is right and extend mercy to the poor that perhaps this would help him stay the hand of judgment and bring the needed humility that he lacked into his life. Daniel had a heart that he was looking toward the king's welfare. He didn't want to see the king suffer; he wanted to see him do well. Daniel's counsel wasn't a violation of expressing the heart of God to the king. He interpreted the dream accurately and then he also provided godly counsel. When you consider what Daniel did, and then what Jonah did, when they both were given a heavy message of judgement to deliver, you can see there was a huge difference taking place in their hearts.

What amazes me about the story of Jonah was the great opportunity he missed because of not entering into compassion. When the people of Nineveh heard the message of judgment, the king took it upon himself to give counsel to his people to humble themselves, pray, repent, and cry out for mercy. Amazingly the people did just that and God had respect unto their choice and stayed his hand of judgment for a season of time. The message that the king gave the people should've been part of the counsel that Jonah gave. But, because of the place of his heart, Jonah didn't enter into that opportunity.

Then after the people had repented you could say that this city was in the place of being very teachable. They were broken, they realized the error of their ways, and they were in the place of change. What an awesome time for having a prophet and a teacher to speak to this nation. Not only did the people humble themselves, but the king did as well. Perhaps if Jonah had a heart to teach, he could have changed the whole course of that nation at that time. How many times do we run across a person or a people group who have come to the place of humility before God that they're willing to change? It's such a God moment; a time where the supernatural life of God can enter into a people.

But Jonah couldn't see the opportunity before him because of the anger of his heart. Where did this anger come from? The Bible doesn't really tell us, but it does illustrate to us how important it is that we allow God to help us with our weaknesses. This character flaw frustrated the plans of God to bring a people into repentance and I think perhaps have an impact on their destiny.

The Ninevites were ready to be taught at this moment in their history. But yet, there was no teacher. Jonah was the one called into this divine moment in time but he couldn't step into it because of offense and the lack of compassion. Nineveh had a short respite of grace because of their repentance, but I believe God had more in mind for them than just a brief pause in judgment. If Jonah would've begun to teach and preach in the city who knows what righteousness could've sprung up in the Syrians. I do know there is a time where the Syrians are going to be called the friends of Israel. It's prophesied in Isaiah chapter 19. So the heart of God is to bring this people group to a place of righteousness.

Giftedness is wonderful and it's one of the vehicles that God uses to reveal his kingdom to those in darkness. But godly character is just as essential. We shouldn't place emphasis on giftedness over character. Instead, we should encourage the maturing of both together. One without the other is disastrous.

Jonah didn't want mercy for Ninevah. Jonah wanted judgement. He wanted this country to pay for its wickedness. In one sense God agreed with Jonah. God agreed that something needed to change. But God's methods were different than Jonah's. God was trying to answer the concern of Jonah's heart, but using a different approach. And He invited Jonah into a transitional moment in history! I like to think of it this way, God was inviting Jonah into becoming the answer for the concern of Jonah's heart regarding Ninevah and the safety of Israel.

Jonah's impact on history could have been powerful! But anger stood in the way. God asked Jonah, do you do well to be angry? The answer is obvious! Absolutely not! What would have happened to Ninevah had Jonah preached righteousness in this city?

What is God inviting you to? What character flaws are standing in the way? It's so worth yielding to God. The consequences are so great. God will help you. He's not looking for perfect vessels but willing ones. Ones that are willing to be molded, willing to let go. Ones who are willing to changeAnd, willing to love.

A prophet is always being tested in ministry. Walk softly in the prophetic before God. And be sure to check your heart. Am I operating in love and compassion toward the person I'm prophesying to? If you're not sure of something, then hold onto it instead of releasing that word. In the context of local church ministry, most prophecy can wait a day if not longer. Take time to pray, because you can always come back to it. And finally, consider the deeper meaning behind what God is saying. God sent both Jonah and Daniel, but only one of these men fully revealed the heart of God through his actions and words.

10 CLOSING

There is a wonderful adventure waiting for you as you explore the many ways God speaks. Prophecy is a vehicle that will propel you into something much more grand than impactful ministry and timely wisdom. Prophecy is a means for God to release His voice in your life and through your life, with the result of being intertwined with Him. You will be propelled into a holy, intimate, and personal conversation that will change you and those you influence. May you be blessed as you pursue what Paul encouraged us to pursue. The joy of the Lord is waiting for your searching heart.

11 PROPHETIC EXERCISES

The best way to grow in prophesying is to practice. It's kind of like riding a bike. When you first began to ride a bike you probably didn't have good balance, and you probably fell over several times. But, as you practiced, you got better at balancing and pedaling. I practice all the time. You can learn how to hear God's voice by practicing.

I have included several practice exercises for you to choose from. Or better yet, do them all. Have fun with it. And enjoy learning. God takes pleasure in your learning. Don't get discouraged when you get it wrong. Remember anything worth doing well requires diligent application and patience in growing. When you miss it, get back up and try again.

If you are really serious about pursuing prophecy, you should set goals for yourself to practice often each week.

Anywhere Exercise

I work in a tall building with several elevators. One of the exercises I do is I ask the Lord which elevator is going to open for me to ride in. Since there are six elevator banks, this makes the exercise more interesting. You can do this type of exercise with almost anything and anywhere. For example, as you're riding down the road and you come to a stop sign or stop light you can ask the Lord what color of car is going to stop right behind you or next to you. I like doing this type of exercise with something that is more difficult than a 50/50 chance of getting it right, that way I know that it is not just chance when I get it right. Another example would be asking the Lord who it is that just called you on the phone prior to you knowing who it is. All of these are examples of engaging with God to ask about routine things that happen in your life and begin to learn how to hear and receive revelation from Him.

Word Exercise

I work with a lot of people in the business world. One exercise that I sometimes do is I will ask the Lord for a word for people I work with. I just ask God for one word, and I will ask him for a person I have in mind. I will then wait on God for a minute or two until I receive a word through the different ways God speaks (through my senses, impression, etc.) When I see this person, I will tell them that I have a word for the day for them. I will then share the word with them. I normally don't tell them that I heard this word from God so as not to offend them, unless I know they are a Christian and then I will let them know. On more than one occasion I have had people tell me that this word was exactly what they needed to hear for the day. But, I don't always get positive affirmation.

You can do this kind of exercise anywhere you are, including the grocery store, school, walking around your neighborhood, and anywhere else you find yourself.

Prophetic Word for a Friend, Family Member, or Neighbor

This exercise is a little riskier than the first two. In this exercise I will purposely spend time praying and talking with God about getting a prophetic message for a friend, family member, or neighbor. I will write down what I receive so that I can hand the message to this person as well as speak it to them.

A good way to approach doing this is telling the person who you received the message for that you were practicing learning how to hear from God. You can then let them know that you had prayed and believed that what you received was something for them. If they are willing to receive what you have to share, then the door is open for you to speak this message to them. If they politely decline, don't be discouraged. You can just take that message and pray for this person in your own time.

After you give them the message, just like in other areas of the book we have discussed, encourage them to seek God about it, to test it, and that if this was from Him, to ask God to reveal more about it to them. Remember, God is drawing and inviting them into relationship with Him through this moment, too.

The World Around You Exercise

God has something to say about everything in life. That includes where you work, where you live, the government, the education system, societal issues, and everything else. Pick one of these areas and ask the Lord what he wants to say about it. Write it down and pray about it. And then watch for God to confirm what you wrote. If you heard accurately, then something will happen to confirm what you had received in revelation. Here is an example of something that I have done in the past, I have prayed and talked with God about hurricanes that were going to hit our country. My heart is to intercede and ask God for mercy. I have also asked Him to tell me what category that hurricane would be when it hit land. He has shown me on a number of occasions what level a hurricane would be several days out from when it was projected to hit land. Obviously, that doesn't work if you are glued to the television and watching every report. I shared this example just as an illustration that you can talk to the Lord about anything. I have talked to Him about all kinds of things including business issues, family issues, governmental issues, and societal events.

ABOUT THE AUTHOR

David Bates is the founder of Trumpet Call International Ministries (TCIM). TCIM is a parachurch organization focused on equipping the body of Christ to fulfill the great commission. TCIM conducts short term mission trips, trains believers through onsite and offsite methods throughout the year, and strategically invests in key leaders in the international community. In addition to TCIM, David currently serves in various leadership positions in two prophetic networks and has been actively involved in church leadership for more than 25 years. His passion is to promote Christian values and culture in all aspects of society, and equip the body of Christ in all the giftings and spiritual blessings made available to us in Christ. David and his wife Michelle are blessed with four beautiful girls and currently reside in Indian Land, SC.

Contact

Email: dcb2019@yahoo.com

Made in the USA
Middletown, DE
31 March 2023

27515269R00056